Arthur Edward John Legge

Wind on the Harp-Strings

Poems

Arthur Edward John Legge

Wind on the Harp-Strings
Poems

ISBN/EAN: 9783744711456

Printed in Europe, USA, Canada, Australia, Japan

Cover: Foto ©Thomas Meinert / pixelio.de

More available books at **www.hansebooks.com**

Wind on the Harp-strings

POEMS

BY

ARTHUR E. J. LEGGE

PUBLISHED BY ARTHUR L. HUMPHREYS,
187 PICCADILLY, LONDON, & SOLD BY
HATCHARDS, AT THE SAME ADDRESS . 1896

NOTE.

I UNDERSTAND that the legend of Rolandseck has been told by Schiller. I have not read his poem, and do not know how he has treated the matter; but, as I may possibly be accused of presumption in laying hands on a subject which his genius had appropriated, perhaps I may say that many English readers of poetry are unacquainted with the German language, and I have ventured to hope that for them the beauty of the story may to some extent atone for my shortcomings in telling it.

For permission to reprint 'The Isolation of England' I have to thank the editor of the *St. James's Gazette*, in which journal it originally appeared.

CONTENTS.

ENGLAND.

My soul is fevered with enchanted wine
  Poured golden from the jewelled cup of spring,
Here, where the hawthorn branches intertwine,
  And, canopied in bloom, the thrushes sing
Concerted seconds to the nightingale
  Who leads this chorus with more copious song
    So sweet and strong
That, further down the vale,
  I scarce can heed the cuckoo's muffled calling,
Or note the plaintive wind's eternal wail
  Over the hill-top, through the pine-wood falling.
A goddess lays her hand upon my heart,
  Touches its drooping chords with unseen fingers,
    Till air, sky, ground,
    Give harmonies of sight, and scent, and sound,
To soothe each aching nerve, to heal the smart
  Where the world's stroke still lingers.

My own loved land of blossom and of bird!
  Once more I come for shelter to thy breast,
Sick of the streets where puny mortals herd
  Through sunless days, whose night is robbed of rest,
  Whose hope drags down, whose joys are all unblest.
    Give me again the right to walk
    Alone beneath a wind-swept sky

Through countless shades of green and tones of
    To watch the wheeling hawk   [yellow,—
    Before resentful swallows fly,
To hear the wood-dove calling to his fellow,
While sky-larks overhead are quivering
    In rapturous madness as they sing,
And sound of lowing kine comes soft and mellow,
    And all this wealth of beauty doth invite   .
    To dream-born revelries of rich delight.

This is our England ! In these woods and fields
    Through long-descending ages has been reared
A lordly brood of warriors, whose shields
    Were bulwarks unto freedom,—who have heard
    High voices calling them,—who have not feared
To walk erect in face of God and man.
    Slow in speech and act and thought,
    Slow, but steadfast, caring nought
Which way the shifting tide of Fortune ran ;
Fighters and workers,—somewhat stern of bearing,
    Lacking, perhaps, the graceful Southern mirth,—
    A little blind to beauty's living worth,—
Thinking their own large share of life the whole.
    And yet of regal birth,
Proud with the manly pride of dauntless daring,
Firm in the liberty of self-control.

Oh wise, strong race ! though jealous fools may sneer,
    Loving to lay their finger on your faults,—
Like one who finds some great cathedral's gloom ·
 · Suggest no solemn hope, no sacred fear,
But only corpses rotting in each tomb
    And skeletons corroded in its vaults,—

However fierce a light be cast
    Across the record of your days,·
You will not need to shrink before its rays,
    Nor strive to cloak your past
From any questioner's observant gaze.
Yours is an heritage of just renown,
    Who still were sane when all the world went mad,
Who have not trembled at a tyrant's frown,
    Nor owned the spell of lawless folly, clad
In specious words with shallow cunning spoken,—
    Guarding your crown
Of truth and honest purpose still unbroken.

Keep you your course along the tracks of time,
    Bearing the stately burden you inherit,—
The shadow of a mystery sublime,—
    The moving power of an unseen spirit,—
        Before no fitful tempest bent,
        In doubt and darkness undismayed,·
From passion's futile thraldom free, nor swayed
        By sickly, sensual sentiment ;
But keeping still untarnished that fair name
    Your fathers won, who taught you to be free,
    Whose star shines peerless through the days to be,
More precious than all store of kingly treasure,
Or music from enchanted isles of pleasure,—
Gift that no price of blood or gold can measure,
    Glowing with rays of a celestial flame,
    Shrined in the depths of an eternal sea.

A LONDON FOG.

THE gas-lamps flicker and flare
  Like restless, straining eyes
Mad with the great despair
  Of a death that never dies ;
Yearning for cool repose
  To freshen their jaded light,
For their eyelids do not close
  In the night.

Out on the green old earth,
  Beyond this shuddering pall,
With a sober, stately mirth
  The temperate sunbeams fall,—
Or the moonlight sips the dew
  In the drifted leaf's brown cup,
And colours the mist anew
  Climbing up.

But here there is no peace
  From the quiver of endless pain,
From the sounds that never cease
  To buffet the air in vain ;
Through the panting giant's lips
  The murmur of anguish moans
As the tortured city grips
  At its stones.

I can hear its fingers scrape
  On its bosom's crumbling skin,
I can see their hideous shape,
  Like the ghosts of gloomy sin,

Flitting along the street
　In the forms of women and men,
Ere the fog's half-lifted sheet
　Falls again.

Jingle, and rattle, and roar !
　It draws its labouring breath,
Sweating at every pore
　With the oozy slime of death.
Its streets are as swollen veins
　Which the throb of its heart-beat loads
With blood that sullies and stains,
　And corrodes.

Its jarring noises seem
　To blend in a piteous prayer
For a break in its ghastly dream,
　A breath of untainted air.
Is the great, strong sun afraid
　To offer so slight a boon ?
Is it idle to ask for aid
　From the moon ?

Yes ! be it night or day,
　No sunbeam rends the shroud,
While the moon is far away
　Asleep on a feathery cloud.
The city may gasp and die
　Ere ever its voice be heard,
Ere the heart of the sex-less sky
　Shall be stirred.

UNDER A STREET LAMP.

A PALE, but blotched and bloated face,
  Ill-featured and unshaven,
With many a deep unlovely trace
  Of lowest life engraven;

Thick, cruel lips, whose parting seemed
  To form a fleshly pocket ;
And one forbidding eye that gleamed
  Dull in its narrow socket ;

A flat, receding forehead, fringed
  With locks unkempt and sandy ;
And cheeks whose native hue was tinged
  With dirt, and blood, and brandy ;—

Thus has the hasty portrait stood
  That Memory's pencil sketches,—
The most repulsive in the brood
  Of London's broken wretches.

I watched your shifting footsteps prowl
  Close to the gas-lit tavern,
And likened you to spectres foul
  In a subterranean cavern.

For, 'mid the varied types that spring
    From mortal man and woman,
'Twere strange to find another thing
    So hard to rank as human.

Noisily down the sloppy street
    A cab came quickly splashing,
With throb of wheels and horse's feet,
    With lights and panels flashing.

It stopped, and underneath the lamp
    A girl, with swift and sure step
That scarcely touched the pavement's damp,
    Glided upon a doorstep.

With one slim hand upon the bell,
    Whose distant voice was pealing,
She turned, and all the gaslight fell
    On face and form, revealing

Great eyes, like dark blue seas that shine
    Beneath the moon's reflection,
Lips rounded in a mould divine,
    A lustrous, pale complexion,

Thick coils of hazy, golden hair,
    Draped on the brow of Venus,—
And you and I stood staring there,
    With one brief bond between us.

A door flung back,—a flood of light,
    Cut short, as the charm was shattered,—
And nothing left but the murky night
    By flaming jets bespattered.

And the joy that stirred my bosom sank
  At the loss of that fair vision,
While my spirit strove to fill the blank
  With a laugh of faint derision.

Was it in some sardonic mood
  Of Fate's predestination
That from such elements was brewed
  So strange a combination?

She, with her purity and grace;
  I, with—well, never mind it;
You, with that God-forsaken face
  And the fetid thoughts behind it!

Well, let it pass! We cannot know
  On whom will rest the stigma,
When Time compels us all to go
  And solve the great Enigma.

· THUNDER-WEATHER.

SILVERY-GREY the clouds, like gauzy pillows,
  Dapple the misty sky, whose darkened sheen
Heightens the contrast of the clear-cut willows,
  Silvery-green.

Silver, and green, and grey the water passes,
  Calm and so sluggish you might almost think
Nothing was stirring save the long-stemmed grasses,
  Grouped on the brink.

These bend and whisper while the wind comes drifting:
  Faint and half-hearted, as some Eastern bride,
Sold without love, her master's curtain lifting,
  Creeps to his side.

Still lies the Sultan-earth; with slumber laden,
  Drugged by the glow of vanished days to rest,
Scarcely awake when the dishevelled maiden
  Moves on his breast.

This is the languid noontide of the summer;
  Bird-haunted copse and glade are songless now,
Only the nuthatch, like a ghostly drummer,
  Taps on the bough.

Though clustered fruit will soon be soft and mellow,
   Yet in the orchards all the leaves are green,
Though every cornfield is a patch of yellow,
   No ricks are seen.

Sound of the sorrow-burdened breezes straying,
   Moans through the branches like a dying breath,
All the great world of life and growth is paying
   Tribute to death.

MIST.

WE walked beneath a sullen, wintry sky,
  Beside a leaden stream,
Whose sound was like some lonely spirit's sigh,
  Awakened by the theme,
The sad old theme the river's whisper taught,
  And poured on heart and brain,
With echoes, from the world's wild voices caught,
Of faded hopes, and dreams, and blighting thought,
  And passion born in pain.

You told me half the burden of your mind,
  And from your tone I guessed
How much of that which lay concealed behind
  Was coloured like the rest.
It seemed to suit the river's mournful song,
  For all its purport showed
That the keen sense of life proportioned wrong,
Of bitter disenchantment tasted long,
  Deep in your bosom glowed.

AN APRIL SONG.

Like eyes, that with luminous fire
   Most eloquent shine,
Reflecting some ardent desire,
   Some phrenzy divine,
Broad sheet of blue waters, where dances
A cluster of glittering lances,
Thou sendest thy wandering glances
   In concert with mine !

Bare boughs, in whose piteous outstretching
   We seem but to trace
Dark lines of laborious etching
   On infinite space,
Though useless your longing to sever
The distance that parts you, for ever
You silently plead, and endeavour
   To meet and embrace !

Shy bird, though the branches be leafless,
   Thou deignest to sing
Thy rhapsody, careless and griefless,
   Which welcomes the Spring !
Soft breezes, like spirits forsaken,
Your passionate whisper doth waken
Deep thoughts which have never mistaken
   The burden you bring.

For, out of the murmur of voices
   Afloat on this earth,
A strain, as of one who rejoices
   In jubilant mirth,
An echo of hymns Cytherean,
Proclaims, with victorious pæan,
How once in the foaming Ægean
   A goddess had birth.

And through the dim shadow of ages
   She cometh once more
To print on our century's pages
   The text of her lore,
To kindle hot embers, now burning
In hearts that are slowly discerning
The strength of tumultuous yearning
   Which moved them before.

We wait thee, expectant and breathless
   With triumph and shame,
Thou queen undisputed and deathless,
   Who comest to claim
Thy power, but half comprehended,
Of passion and agony blended.
Of questions unanswered, unended,
   For ever the same.

SEA-GULLS IN THE THAMES.

GRACEFUL, fearless sons of the sea !
　Stoop and glide, where the falling tide
Hurries its turbulent waters down,
Panting, quivering, stained and brown
With dust and grime of the gloomy town,
　　Like a restless host rushing on to the coast
　　In feverish haste to be free.

What should lead you to linger here ?
　Warehouse walls, on whose squalor falls
Cankering light from a rusty sun ?
Latticed bridges, like webs once spun
By monstrous spiders, whose threads have run
　　In angular links o'er the stream that shrinks
　　From mouldering wharf and pier ?

You should be out on the broad expanse
　Crystalline of luminous brine,
Where fiery Morn with her slim strong wrist
Guides her car through the golden mist
On a gleaming pathway of amethyst,
　　And the sky's bright blue is painted anew
　　And the wavelets ripple and dance.

Seething, frothing, eddies and whirls
  Foam and flake in the steamer's wake,
And labouring paddle-wheels thump and churn,
And brass-bound eyes in the sunlight burn,
And the groaning rudder beneath the stern
    Leaves a lingering line of bubbles, that shine
      Like masses of floating pearls.

Sharply stamped on the ground of blue,
  Dusky red, like beech-leaves dead
In a dark wood, flushed by an autumn glow,
Or white as patches of frozen snow,
The little square sails are gliding slow,
    Ephemeral things, with butterfly wings,
      As daintily feathered as you.

Oh ! my heart goes out to the open sea,—
  Fiercely cries for cloudless skies
And waves that flash in the noon-day glare,
Far from the shadows of social care,
From the noise and strife of this human fair,—
    And deeper than words are my thanks to the birds,
      Who have brought this vision to me.

AT A BAL MASQUÉ.

FAIR partner, I am sick of thought
  And sick of unachieving toil,
Of building hopes that come to nought,
  Of plucking fruit for time to spoil.
I fain would cease to search and probe
  Enigmas that I may not guess,
And Folly's kindly hand shall robe
  My spirit in a fancy dress.

The wail and throb of violins,
  The muffled tread of dancing feet,
Have waked a chord whose music wins
  Soft echoes from my pulse's beat.
Amidst the surging waves of sound,
  The scented air, the brilliant light,
My soul a soothing draught has found
  To drug it into sleep to-night.

And souls were surely out of place
  In such a motley crowd as this,—
Wisdom should wear a fool's grimace
  To yield the laugh we would not miss,—
Gay Fancy should transfigure Truth
  To screen the damaged wares it sells,—
Maturity should mimic Youth,
  And Reason don the cap and bells.

'' How I love life !' you said, and I,
　　Who have not loved it over-much,
Can feel, responsive to your cry,
　　My blood go bounding at the touch
Of your light fingers on my sleeve,
　　Your slender arm against my side,
Till o'er the waves of make-believe
　　Before a buoyant wind I ride.

You, for this waning hour, shall be
　　My heart's delight, my spirit's breath,
The one complete epitome
　　Of all I hope in life or death ;
I'll take the tune of my desire
　　From your wide eyes, and will not ask
What hate or love, what frost or fire,
　　May slumber there beneath your mask.

Yes, life is good ! your curving lips
　　With smiling radiance part and glow,
Your shrouded bosom swells and dips
　　Beneath your drooping domino ;
The lilt of rhythmic motion springs
　　Through the lithe, supple form I press,
And, whirled away on magic wings,
　　We dance into forgetfulness.

C

THE UNKNOWN LAND.

I WATCH deep shades of colour blending,
  As the languid stream goes smoothly by,
Beneath the slope where boughs are bending
  And the willows wave against the sky ;
Great drunken lilies stoop to tipple
  From leafy cups with a crest of foam,
And the faint, faint note of many a ripple,
  Is the voice of nymphs in their reed-girt home.

The jagged edge of a wood, which lies on
  A long, low hill some fields away,
Has cut the rim of a clear horizon,
  A dark green comb on a bed of gray,
That is broken here and there and brightened
  By the pallid sunbeams struggling through,
Whose washed-out gold has almost whitened
  In the thick, damp clouds that crown the view.

The blood is out of the face of nature,
  And her eyes with the wanton tears are wet,
Which have blurred and softened every feature
  In the mournful mood she is wearing yet ;
And the broad green valley is darkly quiet,
  As the slumbrous wind blows moist and cool,
With never a sound save the distant riot
  Of the foaming weir and its frothy pool.

Far from the river my thoughts are taking
  To the edge of the wood their lonely flight,
Where the last faint smile of the sun is making
  The wet leaves flash with a misty light ;
And they pierce the watery curtain closing
  The final scene of an ended play,
And reach at last to a land reposing
  In the gold and green of a perfect day.

A land where no mortal eyes have rested,
  Where no earthly foot has been known to pass,
Where the hills with diamond crags are crested,
  And the dew drops pearls on the gleaming grass;
Not a flower of pain, not a plant of sorrow
  Can scatter seed on the scented air,
For the magic peace of the great To-morrow
  And its rainbow riches are buried there.

Day by day have we hoped to reach it,
  And month by month has the hope proved vain ;
Though the truth has many a fact to teach it,
  We turn and turn to our quest again.
Each morning flashes a look to find it
  On the hazy brow of the furthest hill,
But our land is lost in the depths behind it,
  And the sun goes down from us searching still.

It lay so close to our childhood's garden
  We could hear the splash of its fairy streams,
In the days ere thought had begun to harden,
  Ere the clouds grew dense in our world of dreams.

But we lost our way in the tangled forest
  Which the path of each earthly life has crossed,
And now, when the need of its hope is sorest,
  The sight and the sound of our land are lost.

But our old belief in its sure existence
  Still comes at times when our hearts are faint,
And our fancies float to the dim blue distance,
  Led on by the smiling scenes they paint.
Though doubts may fetter and fears encumber
  Our course as we strive to understand,
We may still be soothed in a griefless slumber
  By the wind that sighs from the unknown land.

TWILIGHT.

THE lights burn red in the mist,
   And the coal-black trees are bare,
And the gleam of the dark, wet street,
And the patter of restless feet
    Seem to grip my heart with a dull despair
      Too strong to resist.

Endless sorrow and pain,
   Labour that leads to nought,
Passion that mocks and lies,
Love that flickers and dies,
    For the fruitless battle must still be fought,
      With nothing to gain.

Why must we darkly grope?
   Why must we labour and fight?
What is the good of it all?
No one hears when we call,
    And yet we never have lost the light
      Of a glimmer of hope.

AN OLD HOUSE.

PEACE of Autumn ! No sound that tells
Of the toil and clamour wherein man dwells,
But a stealthy rustle amongst the leaves,
And the ivy quivering under the eaves
Of the inner court, or waving yet
On the stone of the time-scarred parapet ;
And a pigeon's call blown faint from the wood
Hanging above like a monkish hood
On the hill's broad shoulders, where, to and fro
Reverberate echoes, as pheasants crow
A challenge of right to their roosting-place ;
While from the willows, through which we trace
The course of the stream with its vapour cowl,
Come the plaintive voices of water-fowl ;
And a slow rook, sailing across the sky,
Deepens the chords with a harsher cry.

All around are the woods aflush
With splashes of colour,—the beech leaves blush
On tapering branches, the oaks are brown,
And the birches carry a golden crown

To their stems of silver,—fair forest queens,—
While stripes of variant yellows and greens
Spread up to the rim of the world, and die
On the infinite blue of a flawless sky.
And here, where the flash of the sunlight falls
With a rich, red glow on the darkened walls,
And the panes of the dusky windows glare
Like eyes enfeebled with age and care,
'Twere a pleasant fancy to think there came
Through the mouldering mansion's stately frame
A last, dim flutter of vital breath
Ere its heart lay cold in the damp of death.
And, as before the dreamy gaze
Of a tired woman her early days
Revive in some winter evening's gloom,
When the fire-light flickers across the room,
And scenes come back from the stage of youth,
And the plays are acted once more in truth,—
The loves and conquests, the fierce sweet strife
Of passion and strength and the pride of life,
The hopes and visions, so deep and vast,
All the fair, dead joys of the past,—
So, through the hush of the lonely house,
Where nothing stirs save the moth and the mouse,
Comes a vision, for those who have eyes to see,
Of a long-departed company.
In rooms where the woven hangings rust,
And the floor's dark polish is dim with dust,
Where time's disfiguring stains obscure
The faded hues of the furniture,
Hazy and blurred, like the shadows cast
By the struggling light, from a distant past

Steal spectral faces with mournful eyes,
And the misty shapes of the dead arise,
And wild, sad voices weirdly spring
From the lips of a ghostly gathering.
A moment's fancy !—then nothing more
Than the slumbrous quiet that ruled before ;
The glory dragged from its grave has fled,—
Let us leave the dead to bury their dead.

AMONG THE MOUNTAINS.

HERE, in the hush of the long grey mountain side,
Are the voices calm that were loud in the world below;
The quiver and throb of the turning wheels have died,
And the notes that wail from the kennels of earthly
     woe
Are lost in the roar of the stream's resounding flow,
As it leaps and laughs, with its old mysterious song,
Like a ghostly troop of warriors swept along
Through the thick flakes foamed by the thundering
     steeds they ride.

No further sound,—and, afar from its stony bed,
Where the music fails to strike on the listening ear,
I clamber up to a world where the wind is dead,
Where the silence grows, till my spirit can almost
     hear
The stealthy march of the shadows advancing near
O'er the short, smooth turf, as the sun goes sliding
     down
On a bed of blue to the fringe of the fearful crown
Fashioned by crags on the mountain's slumbering head.

Solemn and vague, through the depths of my shrink-
      ing soul,
Moveth the spell of a stillness worse than sound,
And many a thought that has lived like a toiling mole
In the sightless gloom of its chambers underground
Comes blinking forth, and warily glances round
At this awful space of infinite air and sky,   .
And boldly joins the shadowy dreams that lie
Beyond the reach of a weary brain's control.

Far beneath, in the valley we call the world,
Where scraps of stone through the dark green surface
      break,
We were wont to think them rocks by a Titan hurled,
And the sprigs that stand on the shore of the shrunken
      lake
Were once tall trees, and the square white blocks
      which make
A tiny patch on the carpet here and there,
With a blurr above like a whisp of elfin hair,
Were human homes over which the smoke-wreaths
      curled.

There doth the empire end of the midget man,
Who proudly plays his part in a world of toys,
Who ties the threads of thought in a worthless plan
Of childish hopes and vain illusory joys,
Whom the buzz and hum of his insect race annoys,
And the golden gleam of a grain of sand delights,
Who frets and struts through a few short days and
      nights
Ere his footsteps fade in the mist where his course
      began.

As I gaze and gaze I could almost laugh to think
Of the things whose life is measured by months and
    weeks,
Of the films that are blown at hazard to dance and sink
On the breath of man, ere he tosses them down and
    seeks
The lonely calm of the cold, majestic peaks,
With a wild endeavour to quench the burning thirst
That grips his throat like flame as the bubbles burst
Into shreds, and dry ere the tortured lips can drink.

But the mountain soothes his pain with a wondrous
    cure
As he clings like a child to its vast maternal breast,
Where light and cloud and shadow alone endure,
Where space is a dreamer's vision and time a jest,
Where, year on year, the slumbering ages rest,
As the suns like hurrying meteors sink and rise,
And the stars look down in the dusk with their sleep-
    less eyes,
And the swift moons float through the darkness, pale
    and pure.

As nothing now are the passions whose baneful fire
Have swept from the heart's wide fields the withering
    corn ;
The panting hope and the unfulfilled desire,
The wasted love, the sorrowful, friendless scorn
Have spent their rage, and the soul, no longer torn
Like a wind-split sail, can cover its wounds and
    sleep
In a silent sphere, where only the dewdrops weep,
Where the mists alone can fall and the clouds aspire.

Oh, world of our life of pleasure and toil and pain !
We falter not from the price that your dealers ask ;
Our limbs will bend to carry your load again ;
Our bleeding hands shall finish their fruitless task ;
We will drain the drops that linger yet in the flask,
And shuffle and cut with Time till the cards run
      out ;
We will stand to box with the Fates for a final
      bout,
In the courage surviving hope that is called disdain ;

We will climb the cliff to gather each scented flower ;
We will gird our loins to race for a phantom prize ;
We will serve for fame and folly and wealth and
      power,
For a tinsel wreath and a scroll of flattering lies ;
We will look for love in the gleam of amorous eyes,
And still pursue that flaunting will-o'-the-wisp,
With a fond belief in a flame so clear and crisp,
Though we dare not count on its light for a single
      hour.

But before we turn to follow the path once more
Which leads us back to the life that we would not shirk,
Where the iron must probe our hearts to their inmost
      core,
And gauge their mettle, and prove the powers that
      lurk
To suffer and love, to laugh and wonder and work,
Let us cool our fevered veins in the gentle breath
That blows from the land beyond the river of Death,
With the sound of waves that sob on its tideless shore.

Though the mountain's secret sleeps,—though the
    mists are laid
To cover the curtained glory, fold on fold,—
Though we may not see the Spirits whose steps have
    strayed
On the lonely peaks, whose hair is the sunbeam's
    gold,
Whose eyes shine out of the tarns, whose voice is
    rolled
In the surge and splash of the torrent,—our souls may
    learn
What vastness spreads beyond their vision, and spurn
The Finite's tears and terrors,—of nought afraid.

A HOT-HOUSE PLANT.

OUR worlds are leagues asunder,
  Our lives are years apart,
Through mists of doubt and wonder
  The linked word-flashes dart.
Touched by the glow, we scarcely know
  Where truth begins or ends ;
How far the moods that surge and sway
Are playful storm or stormy play,
  And if we meet as lovers or as friends.

We wear, to ontward seeming,
  The bands of common-place ;
No shade of deeper dreaming
  Reflects from face to face.
Convention's mask and fashion's task
  Would seem to cover all.
Such level ground on either side,
The shortest distance serves to hide
  The gulf across whose gaping rift we call.

You walk within a garden,
  Whose bounds you may not pass,
Where dewdrop sprays are starred in
  A cloth of velvet grass,

Where colour shines in ordered lines
    Of well-trimmed flower-beds,
Where slumbrous scents that poppies bear
Perfume the softly-stirring air,
    And fragrant roses droop their idle heads.

A sheltered, soft existence
    Fulfils your share of life ;
Far in the buried distance
    Lie suffering and strife ;
The weary din of toil and sin
    Sounds faintly to your ears ;
In shaded light your joys are cast,
In lighted shade your griefs have passed ;
    Your laughter makes a mirror from your
        tears.

You watch with gentle pity,
    That scarce can understand,
The squalid, teeming city,
    The barren, lonely land.
You hear the note of anguish float
    Across the sweeter strain,
And wonder, with a dim regret,
Why thus the rope should gall and fret,
    And what the weight of poverty and pain.

But I am of the nameless
    Who pass your guarded gates ;
I share, content and shameless,
    Their hopes and loves and hates.

The motley crowd,—the poor, the proud,—
　The roving paladin,—
The harlot, pale beneath her paint,—
The bloated sot,—the humble saint,—
　In rags or silk I see my kith and kin.

I rise on cars of fire,
　I crouch in drifts of dust ;
I taste the world's desire,
　I gauge its sad disgust.
The path I tread with blood is red,
　And white with driven snow ;
I chase the sound of tramping feet,
I throb with every pulse's beat,
　And all the lore of life I long to know.

From solitude and sorrow,
　From labour and delight,
From every glad To-morrow,
　And every sad To-night,
From death and birth, from grief and mirth,
　From body and from soul,
From grey disease and florid health,
From pining want and strutting wealth,
　I strive to learn the secret of the Whole.

But when the ceaseless riot
　Is over-loud to bear,
I hunger for the quiet,
　The purer breath of air ;
And, for a day, I turn away
　From Heaven, Earth, and Hell,
To dally with the dainty toys,
The twilight hues, the bloodless joys,
　Of yonder land of mirage where you dwell.

A HOT-HOUSE PLANT.

Though passion never answers
   The yearning of your eyes,
And though your world of dancers
   And flowers and butterflies
Must fail to give the things that live,
   Your heart has held for me
A palm-girt well amidst the sand,
A homestead in a dreary land,
   A shaded coral island in the sea.

A RHYME IN A RESTAURANT.

THE glare of hard electric light
Gleaming on tables dingy white,
Across an atmosphere of smoke,
Through which the forms of hurrying waiters flit;—
Piled hat and cloak
Make backgrounds for discoloured chairs where sit
Bohemians,—bourgeois,—all the crowd
Whose voices, strident, loud,
Are mingled with the clash of knives and forks,
The chink of glasses, pistol-pop of corks;
A strange, unlovely din,
Well matched with certain odours of the place,
Where each habitual smell has found a space,—
Tobacco, steaming dishes, fumes of wine,—
Gehenna-fog of cookery, wherein
Perspiring mortals dine.
Surely no heart can find it good to look
On such a picture! Let us take the book
Of life, and turn to some more pleasing page,
Some dainty landscape, some enchanted scene
Upon a brighter stage,
Where harmonies of colour soothe the sense,
And Fancy's gorgeous wing may waft us hence
Into a world, where Beauty once has been.

No, this doth suit my mood ;
I wish not now to brood
Among the shadowy fables of the past.
Squalid reality
Beckoneth here to me ;
I would not linger in the soft light cast
By legendary sunbeams, which outlast
The setting of their sun.
Dead are the flowers in Tempe now,
And dry the magic fount on Helicon ;
Hushed is the Lesbian song, the lover's vow ;
And, one by one,
The silent ghosts have veiled their heads and gone.
The Muses haunt no more their sacred hill ;
Apollo's lyre is still ;
Dryads and nymphs have ceased to roam˙
Amongst the glades of Thessaly ;
Nor flames of kindling altars flare
Across the purple sea,
Where Aphrodite, with her wet gold hair,
Came smiling from the foam.

Robbed of such faded things, I turn
From buried dreams and beauteous lies
To search, with hard, contemptuous eyes,
The unlovely modern scene, and learn
To laugh away this hour that dies.
Fat tradesmen, gasping, over-fed ;
Lean debauchees, with hectic red
Flushing their mottled faces ; girls
Anæmic, pale,—all mouth and curls,
Sham jewellery, and tawdry pride,—
Ogling the flashy shopman at their side.

But why go through the list ?
The one result is still the same,—the same,
And leaves a sense of scorn, repugnance, shame,
Too potent to resist.

But is it that the chords are over-strung ?
Springs this dark cloud from throbbing brain, and
    nerves
By feverish exhaustion racked and rung ?
Drink, and forget such folly !   Wine can give
The glow that wakes vitality, that serves
To colour hueless hope, transfigure thought,
And with its magic multiples of nought,
Make wild solutions live.
'From this old bottle's dusty throat
I can pour a priceless draught,
Red with the blood of an age remote,
When blood was fire, and flashing yet
With the lurid gleam of a sun long set,
And the glitter of eyes, that laughed
As the grape-juice flushed on the dancing feet,
When they rose with a rhythmic beat,
And mirrored the glow on the swart cheeks, fanned
By the swooning breath of a southern land.

Yes, you may drug the brain, and shroud
Life's sharpest lines in a hazy cloud ;
You may shut your ears to each jarring voice,
You may pick the colours to suit your choice ;
But under the painted veil
Is the toothless grin, and the festered sore,
And the worm that eats at the inmost core,
While each clattering tongue but cloaks the wail

Of a heart that builds its own despair
From idle sorrow and selfish care.
For the world is nought but a whitened tomb,
Where Fate, with a scornful laugh,
As it stripped each soul of its plumes, has thrust
A rotting handful of rags and dust,
And has screened the curse of its shameful doom
With a lying epitaph.

Ah, God ! It seems a simple thing for me
Thus to blaspheme humanity ;
But through my scorn the crimson lifedrops flow,
And by my bitter agonies I know
My lot is linked with theirs for praise or blame.
The inglorious woe
That dulls their coward hearts ; the fear ; the shame
Strutting in shamelessness ; the petty greed
For comfort, low delight, and self-content ;
The hopes that on such worthless aims are bent ;
The hard oblivion of another's need ;
The inhuman mockery, the shallow mirth ;
All the dark mudstains of this clogging earth,
Are mine,—are mine indeed !

Oh, Love !
Eternal, infinite Love !
Though far thy hidden dwelling-place may be,
Wrapped in the ghostly gloom that reigns below,
Or lost in distant, purple depths above,
Come to my prayer with thine inspiring glow,
And lay thy hand on me !
Draw back the unsightly curtain that is spread
Over the portal of each shrinking heart,

And let the shrouded secrets be displayed !
Across the home-spun fabric, torn and frayed,
Gleams the pure brightness of thy golden thread ;
In the grey mass of things corrupt and dead
A living hope and holiness thou art.
Heal with thy radiant touch the vision blind,
And, in the flame of everlasting Good,
Dissolve the transient dross of humankind !
Light the pale stars once more, in heaven to burn,
And, by their beams, let doubting souls discern
The unchanging, deathless bonds of brotherhood !

A PARIS DRESS.

YOUR hand was drooped in languid grace
  Across the velvet chair,
And toyed with knots of foam-like lace,
And smoothed the satin's crumpled face
  With gentle care.

And as your fingers idly moved,
  And laid a soft caress
On folds with changing ripples grooved,
You asked me if my taste approved
  Your Paris dress.

A jesting answer on my tongue,
  I turned towards the door
Which showed the wall with roses hung,
The brilliant crowd that swayed and swung,
  The polished floor.

In the first beams of coming day
  The candle-flames were white ;
Beyond the broad, bare windows lay
The sky's expanse of pearly grey
  And silver light.

And through the casement at my side
  I saw the dusky street,
In whose cold depths faint echoes died
Of rich, voluptuous notes allied
  With dancing feet.

The darkened mass of carriage roofs,
　The grating of a wheel,
Some sleepy coachman's gruff reproofs,
The stamping of impatient hoofs,
　The chink of steel,

Made by their contrast deeper grow
　The silence and the gloom
Of that unlife-like world below,
Which served in vivid lines to show
　Our radiant room.

Dim, ghost-like figures, here and there,
　Like shadows crept along,
Sad types of homeless, dull despair,
Who stood to scan, with listless stare,
　The whirling throng.

Then flashed to you my troubled gaze,
　And fell, with scornful stress,
On your white throat with gems ablaze,—
Your strings of pearls,—your diamond sprays,—
　Your Paris dress.

It seemed as though your pride had tossed
　A cruel insult down
To those whose all, possessed and lost,
Would never count beside the cost
　Of that one gown.

And hellish lines of lurid fire
　Appeared to separate
Your hope and health and high desire
From outcasts, trampled in the mire
　By mocking Fate,

And as a flaring badge of shame
    I held your comelinesss,—
Your soft, sweet smile, that went and came,—
Your sheltered life,—your stately name,—
    Your Paris dress.

But, as we talked of life and art,
    By slow degrees I learned
How well you played your thankless part,
How deep within your weary heart
    The brand was burned.

Beneath the veil, so proudly worn
    To screen your self-control,
The bitter strife and anguish born
Of Destiny's defeats had torn
    Your shrinking soul.

Thwarted ambition's hueless dust,—
    Deep scars by Time unhealed,—
Great talents doomed to rot and rust,—
Life's hope in outer darkness thrust,—
    Your smile concealed.

And, laden by the guilty sense
    Of shallow blame bestowed,
My spirit, stripped of all defence,
Offered the humble reverence
    In justice owed.

Like him who brought his priestly lore
    To curse,—and stayed to bless,
I bowed my conquered head before
The robe of martyrdom you wore,—
    Your Paris dress.

SONG OF A TRAMP.

ALL along the dusty road in bright June weather,
  With the broom like flame upon the tangled banks,
While dandelion stalks are crowned with soft grey
      feather,
  And the big dog-daisies stand in snow-white ranks.

High above the ragged hills, where pine-stems taper
  Over oak-leaf cushions, drift the dappled clouds.
All the landscape quivers through a veil of vapour,
  And the sunbeams sink to sleep in golden shrouds.

Far away,—oh, far away, I hear the voices
  Of the glad birds mingled in their sweet-toned strife,
Deep within my veins the throbbing blood rejoices,
  And my heart goes singing for the pride of life.

THE STEAMER'S CALL.

THERE'S a vessel in the river with her furnaces alight,
    And the smoke-clouds pouring free
Through the long, dark funnels, that, before another
    night,
    Will be far on a western sea.
And the busy feet are moving, and the voices sound,
And the engine thumps and rattles as the stern swings
      round,
      And across the clamour falling
      Comes a ghostly summons calling,
   ' Will you out and away with me?'

I can see the swarthy faces of the sunburnt men
    That are gliding to and fro,
And a burst of feeling rushes from the darkened pen
    Where I locked it long ago;
And I hear an ocean thunder far beyond the town,
And my thoughts are carried seaward as the tide slips
      down,
      And my heart is all on fire
      With the bitter, sweet desire
    To respond to the call and go.

THE BEAT OF THE DRUM.

A BLAZE of scarlet, a gleam of gold,
 A chequer of white, and a tinge of brown ;
The tramp and tremor of footsteps rolled
 Through the pale grey street where the windows
  frown.
With a lusty manhood's reckless air,
 In the flower and flush of their youth they come,
Treading in time to the brazen blare
  And the beat of the drum.

The sounds grow faint as they pass away,
 And the boiling flood of the street once more
Blots out, in the rush of a working day,
 The look of a different world they wore.
But a note it is hard to understand
 Seems to linger yet in the city's hum,
And softly throbs from a distant band
  The beat of the drum.

Lost illusions and dead romance !
 I have seen your symbols flickering by,
You have helped me to cast a fleeting glance
 To the land where the dreams of a boyhood die.
Though gold now governs in place of steel,
 And life's work ends in a sordid sum,
Through the blood that springs from my heart I feel
  The beat of the drum.

LOVE'S COMEDY.

IT began, you know, with a jest,
And the end, if we leave it now, will be much the
    same ;—
  A feathery sigh and a fleeting kiss,—
  It could scarce be reckoned a costly game,
  But when souls are the cards, in a world like this,
    Such stakes are the best.

Let me look just once in your eyes,—
As I hold you thus, with your heart-beat echoing mine,
  And your hair so softly touching my sleeve,—
  Under their lashes they darkly shine ;
  In their liquid depths it were hard to perceive
    The burden that lies.

Had I ventured to call it love,—
This passion that looked like foam on a sun-lit sea
  Made but to melt in the dancing rays,—
  How would those eyes have flashed at me
  One glance, like the lightning's lurid blaze
    In the darkness above !

And the laugh of your merry scorn
Would have called me back from the land where I
    may not tread,
  Where the light wind wanders unrestrained,
  And the sun hangs glittering over-head,
  And the fairy flowers are sweetly stained
    With the dews of morn.

To the world of the shaded lamp,
Of costly dresses and daintily·furnished rooms,
  Of pale, dim colouring, cold and chaste,
  Of dusky hangings and faint perfumes,
  Where the velvet touch of an iron taste
    Has impressed its stamp.

Ah, yes !—you are wise I know ;
And if life should seem but a frivolous fancy-ball,
  Where the throb of a lonely heart's desire
  Must be hushed, and a cooling stream must fall
  On the blood that quivers like molten fire,
    It is better so.

For although the whispering night
And the magic moon and the wonderful stars have made
  Our spirits the chords of a dreamy song,
  You creep from my passionate heart, afraid
  Lest the link should break that has held so long,—
    Let us hope you are right !

And so,—though I long to quaff
The Tantalus-wine that Fate in the goblet pours,
  From the fruit of no earthly vineyard pressed,—
  Thus will I lay my lips on yours ;
  Then bury the dream, with a faded jest
    For its epitaph.

UPON THE BRINK.

Upon the brink !—for ever on the brink !
  Through densely twining under-growth we hear
  The dabble of the water, faint and clear,
Above the whisper of the leaves, that shrink
From noon's hot breath ; we blunder on, and think
    To escape the dark confines of doubt and fear,
    To gain the margin of the silver mere,
And in its cooling depths to plunge and sink.

For we are fettered by the world's false creed,
  Which threads its thorny branches in our track ;
Our feet are clogged by custom's binding weed ;
  Our lungs are panting for the breath they lack ;
With halting hearts we labour to be freed,—
  But still the envious brambles hold us back.

STILL WATER.

A LITTLE, limpid pool,
Set, like an opal, in a jagged ring
Of rocks, whose brown, wet surface, glistening
With crystal brine, spreads colour dark and cool
    Beside this paler thing.

And, like a mermaid's hair,
The clustered seaweed hangs in every cleft,
Curled with the ripples that the waves have left,
Daintily combing out the tresses there
    With fingers sweetly deft.

The silent hand of sleep
Rests on the water, and the light-beams blink
As though an eyelid fluttered from the brink,
Whose hazy lashes, the long shadows, sweep
    Across the pool and sink.

And, motionless below,
A few blurred pinnacles have touched the light,
Like moon-kissed tree-tops in a summer night,
And through the veil of dusky green they show
    Dim streaks of faintest white.

Beyond the wall of rocks,
The vast, unresting ocean heaves and sways,
And, grudging to the pool its peaceful ways,
Against the sand-stone portal softly knocks,
    And for an entrance prays.

But still the door is sealed,
And all its anxious asking is denied.
Till the perfection of another tide
Its bell-toned voices must be clanged and pealed
Upon the further side.

Fair Spirit ! who dost show
But seldom on this earth thy gentle face,
Thy wide-spread wings are drooping, for a space,
Above the water, and thy calm doth throw
Its mantle o'er the place.

For one enchanted hour
Imprisoned fantasies may find release ;
The burning throb of heart and brain can cease ;
And, like the perfume of some scented flower,
Is blown the breath of peace.

So rarely come for us
The dreamlike, mystic moments such as this,
When vague sensations that we seek and miss
Quiver across our heart-strings, trembling thus
As at an angel's kiss.

Our life is like the sea,
Where, even in this sunset's deepening glow,
When all the weary winds are sunk so low
That not one ripple moves, eternally
The currents ebb and flow. ,

Few are the havens found
Whose calm is thus unbroken, unassailed,
Where ghostly thoughts, like spectres cloaked and veiled,
May brood upon the fairy scene, when sound
Is hushed and light has paled.

E

In stillness life is cast
As in a mould, and motion doth but seem
The faint reflection of a sunken beam ;
Yon gliding sails are figments that out-last
   The fading of a dream.

The bars are broken down,—
The line 'twixt sea and sky is swept away,—
In purple haze is night confused with day,—
And through the mysteries of death's dark frown
   Life's radiant smile doth play.

Half opened is the door,—
Our vision almost dwells on things unseen.
We grasp at what the great enigmas mean,—
The starry ceiling and the briny floor,
   And all that rests between.

The strife of soul and sense,
The fitful hope, lame faith, and frosty doubt,
The unmanly whimper, the defiant shout,
The opposing blades of thought that foil and fence,—
   All have been blotted out.

We travel on this earth
Searching for something which we never find,
Stung by the smarting flesh and aching mind,
Yet hoping still to rend the cloudy girth
   And reach the light behind.

And man, to suit his mood,
A thousand mixed emotions tastes and tries,—
Takes agonies and raptures, loves and lies,
Hatreds and fears and laughter for his food,
   In every shape and guise.

But all with one intent,
One purpose, which, perchance, he does not know;—
The body's passions, eager blood's hot flow,
And struggling spirit's loftier sentiment
    To this same object go.

    The cravings of the flesh
Are but the blinded efforts of the soul
To gain some outlet from the net's control,
To touch the boundless void through every mesh,
    And to possess the whole.

    As their environment
Will cramp the form of healthy plants, that lie
Beneath some broken mass of masonry,
And boughs are dwarfed, and straining stems are bent
    That pointed to the sky,

    So man's desires will take
The course most clear for them, and clamber round
The shapeless stones that crush him to the ground;
Bark must be bruised, and tender leaflets break,
    Before a vent be found.

    And, since he can discern
But here and there a filtered, straggling ray,
A washed-out gleam, that flickers in the way,—
Small wonder if his night be slow to learn
    How best to reach the day.

    Nor strange that he should think
Each low ambition and each paltry creed
Sufficed to satisfy his utmost need,
And fancy that his soul but asked to drink
    From wells of lust and greed.

Far from this peaceful spot
The crowded cities lie beneath their smoke,
Where patient multitudes of toiling folk
Fulfil the strenuous labours of their lot,
   Each weighted with his yoke.

And all have some design,
Some guiding motive for each conscious act,
Embodied in some hard, material fact,
By which their hearts have laboured to define
   The want of what they lacked.

The harlot and the thief,
The clear-eyed thinker and the drunken clown,
The countless types and samples of the town,
In each incongruous action ask relief
   From that which weighs them down.

Wherever man may turn
His path on land or water, east or west,
The vague impulsion of this fierce unrest
Like flames of fire unquenchable will burn
   And flicker in his breast.

If, rapt in eager toil,
Our limbs grow weary and our senses tire,
The force that urges us to plough the soil,
To splash the page with ink, the wheel with oil,
   Is still this self-same fire.

In Art's most sacred grove,
When our aspiring souls have drunk their fill
Of colour, sound, or form, and felt the thrill
Of mad accomplishment, they merely strove
   To keep their hunger still.

Or when our limbs have lain
In languid ease beneath a purple sky,
Soothed by the sunbeam's kiss, the breeze's sigh,
One single voice has echoed through our brain,
  This same unearthly cry.

And when Love's anguish looks
From eyes o'er which the tangled hair is shed,
And cheeks are flushed, and mouths are flaming red,
Still is the burden of the Sybil's books
  All uninterpreted.

This Life,—this motive force,
Whose impulse grows or weakens with our breath,
Is like some buried stream's mysterious course,
And vapour cloaks its outlet and its source,
  Draped by the hand of Death.

And only now and then,
When Life and Death half-mingle, can we know
How near or far the seething waters flow,
Or cast one glance into the misty fen
  Through which they come and go.

This is that magic hour !
So come, O gentle Death and lusty Life !
A moment's truce has calmed your playful strife,
And both abandon something of the power
  With which your limbs are rife.

Be with me where I stand
Here on the margin of the perfect pool,
And hold me thus in friendship by the hand,
And let me learn the lessons you have planned
  In this your secret school.

My heart doth feel no fear ;
Your arm, O Life, has linked with mine so long.
I will forget your frowns, your smile is dear ;
A little longer would I have you near,
   My brother, brave and strong.

And thou, my sister dark,
Sweet Death, who hast for me no sombre face,—
Lean thy pale cheek to mine, and let me trace
Thy lineaments, and touch thy hair, and mark
   Thy beauty for a space.

Thou holdest all the keys
Of those dim doors that I some day must pass ;
Thou waitest but the turning of the glass
To bid me bow my head and bend my knees
   Upon the dewy grass.

Comest thou late or soon,
Oh, grant me that my course be bravely run !
That I may take thine advent as a boon,
And watch with no dismay the pensive moon
   Replace the jovial sun.

Look now !—the day is dead ;
The sea her purple cloak of dusk has donned :
The stars in mystic characters are spread
Across the sky ; their meaning have I read
   In that brief glimpse beyond ?

A STUDY IN BROWN.

OH, bare winter fields, unlit by a straggling ray
From the sunless sky, spread out like a veil of grey,
O'er a silent world which muses its life away.

You are calling to me with the face of a long-lost friend,
And the warm dark tones, which colour your features,
     blend
In a mist-draped mirror of thoughts that will know no
     end.

And a long, wild wave of memory throbs and heaves,
And heart-strings are touched by the spell that your
     silence weaves
On the breathless woods, still russet with last year's
     leaves.

And the ragged turf is soft to my town-worn feet
In the wrinkled lane, where the grass and the road-
     way meet,—
Till my heart's blank page is dyed with a painting
     sweet

Of the rough brown land, and the paler brown that lies
In the dress of a girl, who recalls to me fairer skies
With her sunbeam hair and the blue of her English eyes.

CIRCUMSTANCE.

THE gas-light gleams upon the stage before us,
    Tranfiguring the painted pageant there,—
The martial lover, with his warrior chorus,—
    The low-voiced lady with her jewelled hair ;—
It seems as though some kindly spirit bore us
    Through this enchanted land where life is fair,
Where on a couch of colour may be lulled
Our senses, in the music sweetly dulled.

But we are severed by the lifted curtain
    From that gay world where Fancy's moonlight falls.
Around us all is darkness, vague, uncertain,—
    Dim, crouching shapes monopolise the stalls,
And dusky galleries behind are girt in
    Pale rings of faces,—much as if the walls
Were lined with portraits from some ancient tomb,
Which show their ghostly features through the gloom.

The last soft line of thrilling verse is spoken,
    The curtain drops upon an ended act,
The spell of Fancy for a space is broken,
    And leaping light shows the vast building packed
With human forms, whose presence doth betoken
    The assured domain of unromantic fact.
The stream of poetry no longer flows,
But voices mingle in the plainest prose.

Yet, as I turn to you, who have been sitting,
   Your elbow touching mine, throughout the play,
I mark the shadow of the dream still flitting
   Through your dark eyes, and watch your fingers stray·
Round your cloak's edge, and know that half unwitting
   Your mind pursues the thing that passed away,—
The phantom of ethereal delight,
Whose charm has held us in its grip to-night.

With eyelids tremulous and bosom heaving,
   Slowly you wake from your absorbing trance,
While one faint sigh betrays your spirit grieving
   For that which fled, and, with a drooping glance,
You mourn the cruel hindrance to believing
   For ever in a world of pure romance,
And ask why Fate should mock you with the pain
Of these unblest realities again.

You think the world a desert,—bare, unshaded,—
   Wherein the false delusive atmosphere
.Plays wanton freaks upon our vision jaded,
   Painting bright landscapes, which our souls draw near,
Only to find the tempting prospect faded,
   And watch the gleaming waters disappear
From burning sands o'er which the sunlight flings
The pale monotony of mortal things.

Ah, yes, for us whom Fate conspires to fetter
   With colourless convention's narrow rules,
Making the spirit subject to the letter,
   Moulding our thought in artificial schools,
It seems at times as if our course were better
   To fly from earthly wisdom, and be fools.
Our hearts are worn with unavailing strife,
Doomed to respectability for life.

Had we but courage for a brief resistance
  Our spirits surely might break loose and find
That land whose aspect mocked us in the distance,
  Where custom's dull restraints no longer bind,
Where we might lead a golden-hued existence
  Amongst the laughing vagrants of mankind ;
Wander away from formal tracks, and be
The gipsy children of Eternity.

Yet must I pause upon a doubtful query
  Before the tender beauty of your face ;—
Have life's hard roads had power so soon to weary
  The feet which tread them with such youthful grace ?
If Paradise were opened to the Peri
  Might it not prove a disappointing place ?
Was the desire for larger things unseen
That old weak worship of the might-have-been?

Though you and I, beneath the ropes that bind us,
  Should strain with swelling hearts to burst the knot,
Some jealous gazer in the Pit behind us
  May now be dreaming of our fairer lot ;
Perhaps his envious fancy has assigned us,
  In a strange drama with a stirring plot,
The leading parts of passion, pathos, love,
And lime-light always on us from above.

Pardon, I pray, the gleam of cynic laughter,
  Which serves to cloak my sad bewilderment ;
Such empty shadows do we hasten after,
  To Reason's cold rebuffs indifferent ;—
Search through this theatre from floor to rafter,
  You might not learn one lesson of content.
Fruit plucked is tasteless, and the hand of each
Stretches towards the branches out of reach.

And I, whom you have taken for confessor,
   Shall prove, I fear, a very broken reed,
Being a most impenitent transgressor,
   In humble ways against the shallow creed
Of commonplace proprieties,—a guesser
   At all dark problems which I may not read.
Leaving dull tomes of learning on the shelf
I puzzle out solutions for myself.

How can I keep you from this hateful slumber
   That droops like mist upon your helpless soul ?
The platitudes are more than man could number,
   Which from the pompous tongues of pedants roll ;
Yet still the same hard agonies encumber
   Our footsteps,—for we may not shirk the toll
Levied upon us by the bandit, Time,
Who leaves us crushed and beggared with his crime.

So soon, so soon, that bitter day doth reach us
   When the full purport of the scroll is read,
When life's forlorn and barren places teach us
   To cease the search for flowers that are dead,
Though faint and broken voices still beseech us
   To gaze upon the withered blossoms shed
Over life's trampled garden, sere and brown,
Where winter's biting breath has dashed them down.

Our widowed hearts recall their childish pleasure
   In things whose old mysterious charm is lost ;
There was a season when we did not measure
   The depth of our sensations and their cost ;
Life seemed a period of golden leisure
   Where Destiny with lavish hand had tossed
Her gifts for us to gather, as we strayed
Down the bright pathway that the sunbeams made.

In those glad years the sky was surely bluer,
  The grass was vivid with a fairer green,
The legends of a by-gone past were truer
  To hearts illumined with a faith serene,
While sullen fogs and angry storms were fewer,
  And moonlight gilded with a purer sheen
The smile of sleeping summer and the stare
Of winter, watchful in the frozen air.

But now no more we gaze with joyful wonder
  On heath and river, meadow, copse, and lane ;
We look to find no goblin treasure under
  The golden load that crowns the harvest-wain ;
We hear no war-horse treading in the thunder,
  No fairy footstep beating in the rain ;
The lightning leaps not from an Angel's sword
Flashing in front of the armies of the Lord.

Must this be, then, our ultimate conclusion,
  That aspirations only court defeat,
That all we loved was born from the delusion
  Of hopes that lie, and memories that cheat ?—
Your eyes are clouded with a sad confusion,
  As thus you turn to question and entreat.
How could my answers help you, since they go
So little further than the lines you know ?

I can but speak of one day I remember,
  Whose gleam yet lives,—and you might think it good
To light your lantern with its glowing ember
  And find, perchance, some trifle understood
That barred your progress ;—it was in September,—
  The sunset flamed upon a German wood,
Where all was silent save the leaves I heard
Rustle so faintly round some roosting bird.

A broken pile of battlements and bastions
   Above the topmost branches reared its head,—
A ruin, haunted with the dim suggestions
   Of eyes that flashed and hearts that throbbed and bled.
The burden of the world's unanswered questions
   In those grey walls and turrets might be read ;—
The stern old castle,—and the tourist names
Scribbled on parapets and window-frames.

But marks of all this modern desecration
   Were hidden, and the hoary fabric grew
Out of the trees that rimmed its rocky station,
   A dusky mass against the darkening blue,
Like some lone figure lost in meditation
   Before the quiet scene, which stirred anew
Faint recollections of the life that hung
About its portals when the world was young.

Towards the tiny valley, cramped and wrinkled,
   The sea of foliage undulated down,
A dull green canopy, where Autumn sprinkled
   The earliest splashes from her brush of brown,
And smoke-rings curled, and lighted windows twinkled
   Amongst the gables of the little town,
Under the time-scarred precipice of crags
From which the curving branches drooped like flags.

And, out beyond, I saw the gentle quiver
   Of dancing waters, and the pale rays shine
On the broad surface of a gliding river
   Which rolled beyond the wood ;—it was the Rhine,—
The father of fertility,—the giver
   Of bending apple-trees and loaded vine,—
The sleepless sentinel,—the guardian stream
That mirrors in its depths a nation's dream.

And over all the fading landscape brooded
　A haunting silence,—an unearthly spell,—
A sense of vague enchantment, that eluded
　The burdened soul on which its influence fell.
No jarring sound of mortal grief intruded,—
　Only the chime of a melodious bell
In the far village, and faint echoes stirred
By children driving home their scanty herd.

And that deep joy, whose old delight had failed me,
　Rose from the silent grave of buried years,
Beneath the mist of ghostly garments veiled me,
　Draping the landscape in a shroud of tears,
And, with its whispered eloquence assailed me,
　Thrusting aside the phantom of my fears,—
Till once again the starry path I trod
To that dream-garden where we look for God.

And on the steps of an eternal altar,
　I made a binding compact with my soul
That doubt no more should lead me with its halter,
　A timid beast of burden, and control
My paces, and my feet should never falter
　In treading onward to the changeless goal
Of lofty contemplation and desire,
And soaring hopes and fancies winged with fire.

But, from whatever substance life could offer,
　Conceptions should be moulded to my will,
And, heedless of the dullard and the scoffer,
　The vague ideal pursued through good and ill,
Which makes us seekers for the fabled coffer
　Of treasure where the rainbow meets the hill
That looms so near before the sun has gone,
Yet, as we walk, is always farther on.

There is no beauty,—so will artists tell us,—
  Beyond the illusion that our minds create ;
If curve or contour, line or light repel us,
  'Tis only that our hearts are fooled by Fate,
Who puts false colours in the picture, jealous
  Of those that, looking through the narrow grate,
See the wide world spread out beneath its bars,
And commune with the silence and the stars.

Oh pilgrim, reaching for a hand to guide you,
  My feet are lame and halting as your own ;
I wander in the drifted sand beside you
  Through dusty darkness o'er the desert blown ;
I have not gained the peace that is denied you,
  And all your toiling anguish have I known,—
After the weary march the fruitless fight,
And then the long sad watches of the night.

But let us break the clumsy cords that tether
  Our straining fancy to this earth, and weave
A floating world of gossamer and feather,
  An airy paradise of make-believe,
And play the childish game of hope together,
  Content to give our service, and receive
No recompense beyond the boundless wage
Of rest within our heart's own hermitage.

For we will clothe our actions with the glory
  Of proud defiance and exalted aim,
And walk through life as in a fairy story,
  And give to every weed a flower's name,
Bearing the banner when our heads are hoary,
  That youth once blazoned with a scroll of flame ;—
And Death may wake us with his trumpet-call,
And prove we were not dreaming after all.

'THE ISOLATION OF ENGLAND.'

NOVEMBER, 1895.

THE wind is hushed ;—the darkness grows ;—
   The fainting moon is lost in flight ;—
Death lifts a sombre hand, and throws
   His clouds across the face of night.
With parted lips and haggard stare,
   That strives and strains to pierce the gloom,
Each nation crouches in its lair,
   And, breathless, waits the coming doom.

Dim, shapeless shadows pass like ghosts ;
   Along the trembling earth they feel
The distant tramp of marching hosts,
   And hear the smothered clash of steel ;
Till, reaching out for friendly hands
   To guide them through the gloom, they press
To where one silent figure stands
   Serene in lofty loneliness.

They hurl their taunts, their oaths, their prayers,—
   The snarl of greed,—the growl of hate ;—
They spit upon the cloak she wears,
   Or grasp its hem to supplicate.

But still, as though she heard them not,
   Her anxious eyes are fixed afar
Amongst the clouds, on one pale spot,
   Where faintly gleams a single star.

By that same star she chose her path
   For every night in vanished years ;
Though screened by mists of doubt and wrath,
   She sees it still,—as if through tears.
Then, glancing at the fretful horde
   Who call her now to bend the knee,
She lays her hand upon her sword,
   And turns her eyes towards the sea.

F

ROLANDSECK.

THE flowing, flaxen hair of Hildegunde !
The great, blue dreaming eyes of Hildegunde !
Like a sweet, slender flower of love she stood
On the grey battlements, as though the wind
Had tossed a floating seed upon the wall
To find in drifts of scanty soil a bed
Between the stones, and, darkly nourished there,
To germinate beneath the sun till time
Drew forth this magic plant. What were the thoughts
That waved across her brain? The vesper light
Moved on her cheek with the reflected blush
Of rose-petals, and threaded through her locks
The gleam of daffodils. Her warm, red mouth
Was curved as though to kiss the coming night,
Whose hand already touched a fairy chord
Upon her heart-strings,—so her yearning gaze
Would seem to promise. High above her head
The banner drooping on the topmost tower
Proclaimed no stirring breath. Before her lay
The vast, unbounded valley of the Rhine
Bathed in a dusky glow ; the purple hills
Stood out in distant solitude ; the fields
Were cushioned with the clumps of trailing vines
Whose load of fruit was green, and, here and there,
A paler patch betokened half-ripe corn.

The mist of sleep was on the hushed old earth,
Shrouding the happy laughter in his face,
And, from the little isle of Nonnenwerth,
The faint, low murmur of a throbbing bell,
Like a pulse beating in the golden air,
Was borne above the stream, and wafted up
Over the peaceful woods, whose foliage made
A bending carpet underneath the rock
Of dusky Drachenfels,—and, climbing yet,
The sound came singing to the maiden's ear.
It was the convent's message to the world,
Greeting the pure in heart,—as Hildegunde.
Her fingers sought the beads about her neck,
And, in the tremor of her parted lips,
Was breathed a whispered prayer. Her fancy dropped
Across the valley like a sinking bird,
And rested in the quiet cloister's shade.
It seemed a pure and holy fate to kneel
There in the chapel with the silent nuns,
And dedicate a human heart to God,
To snap the binding fetters of the world,
To shun the gilded mockeries of life,
And lay her sole and sacred offering
Before the curtained throne. But still she heard
A voice that held her from the sacrifice.
Not yet,—not yet the time for giving all!
God surely had not claimed it! In her blood
There rose a strange unrest ; she pushed the hair
Back from her forehead in a silky mass,
And gazed with pleading, undecided look
Into the gloaming.
           In the wood beneath
The clatter of a toiling horse's hoofs

Rang sharp upon the stones.   Between the trees
A narrow, winding pathway scaled the hill,
Arched with a canopy of bending boughs,
And through the leaves from time to time there flashed
The glint of burnished armour.   Some one came.
The hoof-beats passed the turning of the wall
And softened into silence.   Hildegunde
Waited and watched with languid wonderment.
Soon, by the castle gate, she heard a note
Blown from a bugle echoing down the hill,
To waken voices in the darkened glades,
And ring upon the half-uncovered crags,
And moan and die among the distant peaks.
Then came the warder's challenge, and the stir
And hum of moving men.   She heard her name
Cried out in eager tones, and, hastening,
A damsel sped responsive to her call
With eyes of great import.
                              ' My Lady, come !'
Breathless she said, ' My Lord, your father, waits
Your presence ; they are flinging back the doors,
And all the men-at-arms are mustering
To greet the noble knight.   I heard them say
Such guests were honoured in the Drachenburg,
Claiming our warmest welcome ; and my Lord
Was urgent that your courtesy should grace
The coming of that prince of chivalry,
Count Roland of the Rhine.'
                              Then Hildegunde,
With faintly stirring pulse, and tingling cheek,
Followed the damsel, whose unwearied voice
Went galloping along the course of time,
To make her portrait of the guest complete

Before the moments fled. But Hildegunde
Was busy with her own uncertain thoughts,
Nor marked her empty words, but glided on
With dim forebodings, vague and unexpressed.

Slowly she came into the castle-court
With stately self-possession, that belied
The fierce confusion in her beating veins ;
For all the blood seemed surging to her throat
And throbbing in her eye-balls, till the scene
Grew blurred and misty, with no certain shape
In all the expectant throng, save one small group,
Clear in the shadow of the solid arch
That framed the gaping doors.
                              Count Heribert,—
Lord of the Seven Mountains, noted chief
In battle, far-famed counsellor in peace,—
Came forward with the stranger, who had given
His horse, his shield, his helmet, and his lance
Into the guardianship of serving men
That clustered in the gateway. Hildegunde
Moved on with lowered eyes and shortened breath,
Conscious of one that carried by her side
A cup of golden wine. Her father's voice
Proclaimed her to Count Roland as she took
In both her hands the mighty silver cup,
And offered it, with timid, bending grace.
In courteous reverence the stranger bowed
His goodly head before her ; then he curved
Long, shapely fingers round the proffered cup,
And, ere the draught was lifted to his lips,
Murmured a courtly phrase. His words were light,
But something in their accent brought the blood
Swift to the maiden's face.—She raised her eyes.

One flashing moment in Eternity !
One swift upheaval in a human life !
One gleam of meeting glances !—and the world
Holds something that it never held before.
There, in the shadow of the frowning gate,
While the blue deepened in the darkening sky,
And ebbing sun-beams faded from the roof,
Two spirits woke and mingled.   Face to face,
The silence linked their souls.—Not Heribert
Nor any in the observant groups around
Divined what deep emotion underlay
Their cold formality ; but Hildegunde
Knew nothing save the spell of searching eyes
That seemed to look into her inmost heart
Out of an eager, strong, yet gentle face ;
And Roland's brain was drugged into a dream,
Robbed of all clear sensation, save the joy
Of drinking in such loveliness, and giving
His voiceless homage to the pure, white girl
Whose presence seemed to fill the swooning air
With fragrance, like a breath from Paradise.

That meeting was the prelude ; from its chords
Long, subtle harmonies were woven then
To mingle in such music that all life
Became one sacred symphony ; the hours
Passed in an ecstacy that almost reached
The bounds of earthly passion.   Day by day
The wind was loaded with a fairy song ;
The sun-beams bathed them in an atmosphere
Of soft enchantment ; the congenial woods
Made silence for them with their magic hush ;
And every flower joined in the design
To build a couch of odour-laden air,

Whereon their burdened senses might be steeped
In balmy slumber.   As the days rolled on
The rumoured secret that had gone the rounds
Of the castle gathered strength and certainty,
And men were glad that such a noble knight
Had plucked the lily from their garden-wall
And laid it in his bosom ; Hildegunde
Was Roland's promised bride.
                          His spirit moved
O'ershadowed with delicious wonderment
In acting this new part.   He was a man
Whom Fortune's eyes had ever smiled upon,
And he had made a play-ground of the world,
And taken life as one long holiday,
Fighting or revelling, in toil or sport,
With here and there a little careless love,
But all in lightest mood ; for no long time
Had he sustained resentment in his thoughts,
Or recollection of an idle kiss,
And ever with a cheerful heart had roved
The country-side, on chance adventures bent
As fighter or as lover.   But a change
Had stirred his inmost nature when he walked
Into the fairy home of Hildegunde,
And found the palace of his heart's desire.
For love had fashioned in his soul a harp
And played its elfin music, day and night,
Half mocking at the sweet familiar strain
That ends so often in a broken chord.

Time rippled on in waves of happiness,
And with its stream the lovers drifted down
In blest oblivion, while the long white fringe
Of mist upon the sea of wedded life

Grew clearer on the horizon ; soon their bark
Would float beneath its canopy and cross
The wide mysterious waters ;—Vain belief !
Destiny's hateful pilot was on board,
And steered a sudden passage to the bank.
For, one day, to their idle dream-land came,
A message that eclipsed the wanton sun,
Filling their souls with darkness.   Charlemagne
Sent forth a summons to the faithful knights
That owned allegiance to himself and God,
Bidding them leave their worldly heritage
For duties of diviner origin,
And hasten once more to the Holy Land
Where still the Heathen held the tomb of Christ.

Most piteous was the maiden's flower-like face
When Roland's faltering accents told the doom
That mocked their hopes ; yet no repining word
Constrained him from his duty.   Her wide eyes,—
Deep ocean-pools of blue,—let not the tears
Steal o'er their fringing boundaries ; a smile
Played like a sun-beam on her trembling lips,
Across the cloud of grief ; and, though her hands
Clung tightly to his arm, their pressure gave
No thought of a desire to hold him back.
Nor swerved his mind.   There was a wealth of words
In the grave silence of his marble face,
And in the grip that clutched her to his heart
A fervour of emotion welling up
Out of his burdened soul.   But in their hearts
No doubt had ever stained the simple faith,
Whose truth seemed certain as the daily course
Of cloud and wind and waterway ; for them

Religion was a force apart, above.
The common accidents of earthly life
Were things not reckoned in its holy sphere,
And the faint murmur of the Decalogue
Was lost beneath the thunder of the Creed.
Oh, plainer was the Problem in that age
When Thought went out along a hardened track
Lightly to solve the Eternal Mystery !
The tone and temper of the obedient saint
Had held but little part in Roland's life
Of reckless, hot activities ; and yet
The transit showed to him and Hildegunde
A sequence natural as dark to light,
That he should bind the Cross upon his breast
And march beneath the banners of the Lord.
And so, while yet within the maiden's mind
Thought danced a devil's dance, till every shape
Was vague amidst the throng of whirling limbs,
And life was a delirium like the dreams
That surge and shiver in a drunken brain,
There came a sudden calm, stiller than death,
Wherein she woke, and learned that all was done,.
That she was left before the castle gate
Staring with helpless eyes into the mass
Of corruscating leaves and twisted stems,
Whose shade had blotted out the man she loved :
Leaving her nothing but her solitude,—
His faint voice buried in her frozen heart,—
And, on her flaming mouth his branded kiss.

Days grew to weeks, and weeks to weary months,.
And months began to gather into years ;
And life, with motion imperceptible,

Like glaciers shifting on a mountain-side,
Drew down towards the Valley. ·Far away
Beneath the scornful, tearless Syrian sky
'That seemed to mock, with its unchanging face,
The intruding host of Christians, Roland dwelt.   -
Amongst the stalwart soldiers of the Cross
His fame grew daily ; on each battle-field
His plume and pennon led the fiercest charge ;
And swarthy, nimble Saracens went down
Like grain before the reaper, as he rode
Across the burning desert.   They would look
For the wild knight upon the great brown horse,
With crimson nostril and foam-fretted flanks,   .
As for the sandstorm of their native plains,
A scourge beyond the help of human power,
Hateful and yet sublime.   When the first flame   `
·Of wondrous Eastern mornings leaped and glowed
Along the opposing armies, quivering
In hot, white flashes on the countless points
·Of burnished steel, and blended in the dance
Of streaming banners, tossing manes, and hoofs
That twinkled through the dust,—on Roland's mouth
A passing smile could curve the rigid lips,
And, from the glitter in his stern, sad eyes
'The throng of careless comrades guessed the thought
'That leaped across the continents, and took
From one lone watcher by the silent·Rhine
An impulse that would nerve his hungry heart
'To something higher than their reckless mood
·Of honest courage.   He became for them
'The symbol of that undefined ideal
'Whose spark yet flickered in the gloomiest soul ;
And, though the blunted sense of some might find

Occasion for the comment of a sneer
In his retired and unconvivial moods,
From many a rocky, rugged heart there flowed
A little silent stream of sympathy.

When the rapacious hand of conquest broke
The seal of sheltered harems, and brought forth
Spoil for the victors, he, with cold disdain,
Would waive all right to share ; others might choose
Their scarce-regretful victims from the throng
Of soulless Eastern women ; not for him
Were heaving bosoms and voluptuous shapes,
And rich ripe mouths that trembled with desire,
And all the sensuous harmonies of flesh.
Hereditary wantons, they would yield,
With half a sigh for lovers that were lost
And more than half a smile for lovers gained.
But Roland met the laughter in their eyes
With grave, cold courtesy, that sent a shade
Of wonder o'er their shallow, sparkling minds,
And kept his lonely faith with her he loved
In silent contemplation.
                              O'er the leagues
Of wave and woodland, mountain-crest and plain,
And scar-like valleys and excrescent towns
Their falcon-spirits passed in wheeling flight ;
But distance found them fainter on the wing,
And Time gave force to his hot slave, the sun,
Who beat upon the waxen joints of Hope,
While salt and bitter waters of despair
Were swelling to devour them. Hildegunde,
Galled with the burden of enchaining hours,
Grew white and wearied in her far-off home,

And faltered through the wilderness of life
With lips that thirsted for the wells of Love.
But time crept on, and Roland came not back,
And never golden word of tidings broke
The grey monotonies of grief.   At last
A whisper fluttered to the Drachenfels,
Like a faint pigeon coming home to die
With news beneath its wing.   And all too soon
Hard repetition followed.   Hildegunde
Kept the weak fire of doubt alive when first
The scattered drops of cold, wet rumour fell
Hissing amongst its embers ; but e'er long
The drops became a deluge, and the flame
Faded and sank in darkness, while her heart
Stood shivering beside its ashes, bare
Beneath the blotted sky.—There was no hope.
Roland had fallen.—He was dead,—was dead ?

Like a dim ghost upon the castle-wall
Under the stars she stood.   The magic hush
Of warm, still sleep was in the voiceless air,
And o'er the bosom of the spell-bound earth
Was breathed a languid sigh of fragrant wind,
Heavy with odours from the folded flowers
And freshness of the dew.   Her eyes looked out,
Dark, burning jewels in the dusky night,
And scanned unheedingly the silver path
Of pallid moonlight o'er the clustered leaves,
And watched the broad, white riband of the Rhine
Broken by shapeless islands, and beyond
The shadowy vagueness of the tree-clad hills.
Then, with clasped hands and moving lips she strained
Her sight towards the distant convent, lost

In dense obscurity, and spoke this prayer,
While round her danced and fluttered in the gloom
A gleaming moth, with wings like thistle-down.

'Oh, Mary,—Mary,—Mother of our God !
Thou too hast suffered ; Thou hast known the weight
And anguish of bereavement ; Thou hast seen
Thy Best-beloved taken, and, although
Thou knewest that He was not mortal man,
That sight drove deep into thy wounded breast
Before the Glory touched it.   I have lost
That which had made my heart into a throne
Where earthly joy sat crowned.   The tinsel pomp
Has faded, leaving but a robe of rags
To hide my shrinking nakedness.   I come
Ruined and robbed to kneel before Thy feet.
Oh, spread Thy garment now to cover me !
And let me hide beneath its friendly folds,
And in the cool, sweet shadow dull the pain
That burns into my bosom !'
                              And the moth
Just brushed against her pale face, hovering
As if to take her message, and passed on
Over the wall, and, with its faint white wings,
Vanished amongst the moon-beams in the wood.

And soon the maiden followed, far from men ;—
And in the cloister dwelt another nun
Beneath the trees that whispered o'er the Rhine.

But the mysterious Power that shapes the course
Of human lives had woven once again
A cruel tangle from the knotted threads,
Perhaps in all the ironic bitterness

Of angry scorn, perhaps with deep design
Of future consummation perfected
Far from the reach of limping mortal thought.
Ere yet another spring had flushed the trees
With dainty films of verdure like a cloud
Of pale green gauze, along the winding path
Rode, as before, a solitary knight
Who halted at the gate.   Old Heribert
By chance was with the warder, and looked out.
Then from his lips there came a startled cry,
And o'er the waters of his soul there swept
A gust of dark emotion and dismay.
Like one who labours with a dream, he saw
The face of Roland,—Roland living yet,
And come to claim his bride.   Count Heribert
Had seen the world's raw wounds, and felt the throb
Of anguish beating in its swollen veins,
And tasted of the foul and brackish pools
That fringe the paths of life.   His feet had toiled
Over rough places, and his heart had known
The stab of sorrow, the constraint of care,
The burden of authority, the weight
Of melting vigour and declining years.
He was familiar with the frown of death
And discipline of danger ; but throughout
The tasks and trials of his earthly doom
Nor pain nor loss had struck so hard a blow
As this encounter.   Pitiful enough
Was the mute greeting of these hapless friends ;
For Roland read the meaning of his look,
And silence told the tale.   When voices broke
The spell that gripped them, brief and clumsy words
Filled up the yawning gaps that time had left

In the sad sequence of their chronicles.
With worn, white faces, bloodless lips, and eyes
That shunned the gaze they questioned, each in turn
Picked up the threads and straightened out the coil.
Roland had walked upon the shores of death,
And lingered in the shades of sickness, crushed
With well-nigh mortal wounds.   When Fate had turned
The balance in his favour, and brought back
His soul from that dark region, he had sped,
Still weak and nerveless, to his spirit's home,
Flushed with the strength of hope, to find at last
An old man quavering his mournful news,
A dream-land laid in ruins, and the blank
Of helpless disappointment and despair.

Brief was his sojourn in that fatal house
Of mocking memories.   Awhile he moved
In speechless, tearless anguish through the scenes
Of unforgotten happiness, and strove
To calm the fever which had filled his brain
With wild, sad thoughts, and half delirious doubts,
And ghoulish fears that left him on the brink
Of madness worse than death.   Some time he strayed
Among the relics of his lost delight ;—
The rooms that she had dwelt in, with their store
Of dainty trifles ;—the secluded nook
Where she would watch the sunset from the wall ;—
The flowers her love had tended ;—and the space
Of white, stone floor whereon she knelt in prayer.
There was so little,—yet it held so much.
Then, with a face that seemed to copy death,
He dragged his listless limbs towards his steed
And climbed across the saddle.   Old Heribert

Uttered no faint remonstrance, but stretched out
A trembling hand, and looked into his eyes
With helpless, dumb compassion.　All around
'The winter twilight came in noiseless waves
And in the hushed air there was the taste of frost,
But not one sound.　With laboured self-control
The farewell past between them ;—just a word
In false, light tones that veiled a conquered sigh,—
A grip of hands,—a firmly governed gaze
Charged with well-acted cheerfulness,—a droop
Of eyelids falling as the strain relaxed,—
And Roland turned again into the dusk.
A little while they heard his horse's feet
Tramp on the stones, and watched his shape grow dim
Among the leafless trees,—then all was blank,
And on the castle fell the frozen night.

With silent steps and ever-changing face
The musing year stole onward, while the frown
Of winter melted out of Nature's eyes,
And leaves began to split the russet coats
That cased their nakedness, and starry flowers
Gleamed through the dew-drops in the brightening
　　grass,
And birds were fluting their melodious love,
And woodland whispers brought the fragrant smell
Of rich damp earth.　Then on the timbered slope
That crowned the winding channel's further edge,
Was seen a daily movement like the stir
Of bees amidst a garden ; clear and faint
The sounds of toil were echoed o'er the stream ;—
The shock of sundered stem and wielded axe,—
The grating gasp of saws,—the muffled beat

Of distant hammers,—and the steely chime
Of chisels biting on the blocks of stone.
Barges and rafts were moored beside the bank,
And busy sails came creeping up and down
Like birds that carried strips of water-weed
To twine into their nest. The country rang
With legends of the castle to be built
By Roland, there upon the lofty ridge
Nearest to the island where the Convent lay.
Slowly the solid walls began to lift
Their heads above the tree-tops; arch by arch
And line by line the fabric shaped and grew.
Tower and bastion, battlement and keep,
Buttress and plinth and gable seemed to form
Their substance from the floating river-mist
And frown across the waters. Till one day
The castle in loveliness completed stood
Beneath a sun which glittered on its walls,
And flashed from every pinaret and peak.

And Roland, who had watched the daily toil,
Dwelling amongst the toilers,—who had seen
The stately buildings grow beneath their hands
As he designed them, like the unruly chords
Conquered and trained to noble harmonies
Majestic in some great musician's mind,—
Now reached his journey's end. The noisy crowd
And hum of labour passed like melting snow
Down the broad river. Save the modest troop
Of stern and faithful soldiers, who sufficed
To ensure the castle's safety, he was left
In solitude abiding. Then began
A life that linked him with the world of dreams.

G

Long, lonely hours were passed in silent prayer
And secret warfare fiercer than the strife
Of all his earthly battles.   In his soul
The conflict swelled, unceasingly sustained
By wounded Faith against the bitter doubts
Born from the whirlwind that had wrecked his hopes,
And, night and day, he strove to crush the thoughts
That flung defiance in the face of God.
The contest left its scars upon his face
In furrowed wrinkles round his hollow eyes
That glowed with sunken fire.   His youth was dead,
The power and grace of early days destroyed.
His haggard features and despondent air
Haunted the minds of men who could recall
The laughing, reckless soldier ; and the change
Had stirred the deepest currents of his blood ;
For all his life was in the ways of peace,
And governed by constraining rules, austere
As any anchorite's.   The lonely hut
Wherein the silent woodman shunned the gaze
Of this hard world,—the cottage on the hill
That shrined some timid household's hopes and fears
Under the friendly trees,—the quiet home
Of toiling priests who dwelt among the poor,
Believing that such company was meet
For those that lived near God,—such was the ground
Whereon he spent the vigour that for years
Had asked a fiery outlet,—and he gained
The priceless recompense of grateful hearts.

But all his recreation was to stand
And gaze across the moving water-sheet
To the green island and the convent walls.

When the pure gleam of morning crowned with gold
Clamorous wavelets, and the drooping trees
Swung to the cadence of the rhythmic dance
That swayed their leafy branches as they dipped
Into the burnished flood,—when varied stripes,
Reflected from the canopy of clouds
That caught the splendour of the sinking sun,
Stretched o'er the glassy surface, and the trees
Were dark and still against the dusky sky,
Planted knee-deep in floating waves of mist
That showed transparent on the purple shades,—
And when the languid hush of drowsy night
Lulled the warm bosom of the breathing world,
Whose blotted features took fantastic shapes
Till branch and crag and building were confused
In one blurred mass, that left no form distinct
Save the pale pathway where the waters ran
Mingling the yellow radiance of the stars
With white milk of the moon,—the sleepless eyes
Of Roland kept their vigil. He had learned
The daily course of labour, prayer, and rest,
That passed within the convent. When he heard
The silver chiming of the chapel bell
His sight would strain toward the distant throng
Of hooded nuns, and single out a form
Which veil and hood were powerless to hide.

The chain of woven fancies seemed to stretch
Further and further, while his spirit climbed
Along this unseen bridge across the gulf
That yawned between them, till at last it scaled
The convent wall, and leaped upon her breast.
And daily grew the imagined intercourse,—

The ghostly kiss that hovered on her mouth,—
The pleading voice that whispered in her ear,—
The touch that trembled on her silky locks.
Within the very bounds of Paradise
He boldly walked, and hotly claimed to share
The secrets of her life.   His soul with hers
Wandered in meditation through the paths
That crossed the peaceful garden ; at her side
He paced in dreams the cloister's paving-stones ;
And, when she knelt upon the chapel floor
With soft light floating through the coloured glass
To bathe her in its glory, while around
The pealing organ-music swelled and surged,
His heart was conscious of her ecstacy,
Beating with like devotion, till the chains
Of earth and flesh seemed broken, and they soared
Upward together to the feet of God.

And, as the long days passed, within his breast
The turmoil waned and faded ; slowly sank
The devastating waters of revolt
Out of the flooded garden of his heart,
Till the bruised flowers of life again could lift
Their draggled heads.   Those waters were not stained
With that dark substance which has fouled the stream
Of modern discontent, and given it power
To poison all it touches when the waves
Break out beyond their banks.   He had not known
The bitter desolation and despair
That lays its hand upon our tired souls
As, 'mid the ruins of our earthly joys,
We stand and gaze into the leaden clouds
Which cloak the sky, nor catch one sickly gleam

Of sunlight on the wasted world of thought,
And wonder if there shines a sun at all.
His heart's rebellion was no complex war
Of fettered instincts and unruly blood,
And reason cramped and blinded in the folds
Of dark philosophies,—dim forces joined
To burst the meshes of dishonoured creeds
And struggle on to freedom ; he but knew
The fitful passion of a thwarted child
Who frets at irksome government and rule,
But questions not the source from which they spring.
Thus, then, his heart grew weaker in revolt
And stayed its useless struggles, till beneath
The twilight calm of aspirations dead
And hopes resigned and Fate confessed supreme
He found—not happiness, but bloodless moods
Of ghostly, pale content. From time to time
His body cried in protest impotent
Against the conquered soul ; his veins would throb
With helpless yearning for acknowledgment
And satisfaction of his mortal love ;
But soon the stormy gust would pass away
To leave the troubled waters it had scourged
Sinking in sullen apathy to rest,—
A grey, cold ocean, where the shrouded sun
Woke the faint semblance of a mournful smile.

And time brought clearer vision, till he reached
Something of that deep truth which underlies
The shadows of existence. More and more
The soul transfigured and transfused the flesh
Under a veil of fancy that concealed
The fictions men call facts. Across the gulf

Of time and tears the enchanted bridge was laid,
And in the golden garden of sweet dreams
He lived his wedded life.   No change could mar,
No cloud of disillusionment destroy,
That perfect union.   Soul entwined with soul
In bonds that never chafed, in linked delights
Out of the reach of galling human care,
Of sorrow, sickness, and satiety,
And all the thousand petty blots that stain
The page of earthly passion.   False or true,
The vision never failed him.   Year on year
Went rolling into silence, swept along
Towards Eternity, but time and age
Were powerless to quell the fire that burned
In that lone breast.   His life remained a dream,
Perhaps a long delusion ;—who can tell ?
At least he gained what others ask and miss,—
A strong set purpose,—an abiding calm,—
An empire undisputed in his soul,—
The starry radiance of a quenchless love,—
And hope that looked for an unclouded dawn.

London : STRANGEWAYS, *Printers.*

www.ingramcontent.com/pod-product-compliance
Lightning Source LLC
Chambersburg PA
CBHW020040030726
47499CB00007B/2509